Waiting in Wonder for EASTER

FAMILY DEVOTIONS FOR HOLY WEEK

Written by GAIL PAWLITZ

Illustrated by EVA VAGRETI

CONCORDIA PUBLISHING HOUSE • SAINT LOUIS

In thanks to God for the love
and support of my husband, Ron.
Together, we've shared seasons of
marriage, the joys of raising five
children, and the rewarding
work of teaching the faith.

Copyright © 2018 Concordia Publishing House
3558 S. Jefferson Avenue, St. Louis, MO 63118-3968
1-800-325-3040 · cph.org

Written by Gail Pawlitz

Scripture quotations are from the ESV® Bible (The Holy Bible, English Standard Version®), copyright © 2001 by Crossway, a publishing ministry of Good News Publishers. Used by permission. All rights reserved.

Hymn texts with the abbreviation *LSB* are from *Lutheran Service Book*, copyright © 2006 Concordia Publishing House. All rights reserved.

Manufactured in Shenzhen, China/022100/300680

1 2 3 4 5 6 7 8 9 10   27 26 25 24 23 22 21 20 19 18

Jesus is the victorious Lamb of God, who takes away the sins of the world.

INTRODUCTION

For many children, Easter is about candy, bunnies, more candy, and egg hunts. Those things are fun. But this year, make sure Easter is about Jesus, God's Son, the Lamb of God, the Savior of the world. Since you have chosen this resource, you are already planning to do that.

Begin using these devotions and activities right before Palm Sunday. Each two-page spread includes a devotion, an extra tidbit, a Bible verse or verses, something to do, a prayer, and artwork that will bring meaning to the words. Take plenty of time to savor them. Ask questions. What is Jesus doing? What are God's people today doing? How are some of the illustrations changing? This book will help you teach basic truths. Children already

know about bad things and sin. But you want them to learn and believe so much more. So, it's good that you teach them about God's plan to forgive sins and His plan to send Jesus, who took the punishment for sin. You want them to know that Jesus died on Good Friday but is now alive. And you want them to find comfort in believing that through faith, they are never separated from Him.

As I worked on this book, I prayed that God would bless you through it. And now, I am confident He will. May the events of Holy Week and Easter help you and those you love to appreciate and celebrate Jesus, the Lamb of God, victorious and reigning.   —The author

I wonder, what do we do in Lent?

Do you ever just sit and think? Maybe you wonder which super power you might like to have. Or maybe you look at the sore on your knee. Maybe you wonder what Lent is and what we do during Lent.

Lent is a time before Easter to think and to do. It is a time to pray and to show God's love to others.

Long ago, Jesus spent forty days in the desert. He was thinking about sin. And He was thinking about showing love. He was praying about how to be our Savior. But He was not alone. The devil was there too. He tempted Jesus to sin. But Jesus never sinned; not once, not ever.

After His time in the desert, Jesus chose disciples, did miracles, and taught people about the kingdom of God. And a few years later, He died on the cross for the sins of all, including you.

What can you do during Lent?

You can tell God you are sorry for your sins. That is called confession. You can do acts of love. That is called serving. And in the days ahead, you can read the devotions in this book. That is called fun.

4

Find Out More

What color does the church use in Lent?

Purple (or violet) is used during Lent. The purple cloth reminds us to repent. Right before they nailed Jesus to the cross, the soldiers put a purple robe on Jesus and made fun of Him. Jesus suffered this and many other things so that we might be His own—saved and free.

Say It *[God] is gracious and merciful, slow to anger, and abounding in steadfast love.*

Joel 2:13

Do It Eat pretzels shaped like twisted knots. They look like arms crossed in prayer. When you are done eating, fold your hands in prayer.

Pray It Silently confess your sins to Jesus. Tell Him what you have done wrong. Say you are sorry. Then use one finger to draw a little cross on the palm of your other hand. Remember, God will forgive you because of Jesus.

I wonder, why did people call out "Hosanna" to Jesus?

When you hear someone call "Help, help!" you know that person needs a rescue. Long ago, when Jesus rode into Jerusalem, people stood and cheered. They called out a word like "help." They used the word *hosanna.* It means "Save us, Lord!"

That day, the cheering crowd wanted Jesus to help. They wanted Him to be their king. They wanted Him to get rid of the bad rulers and stop the bad rules. After all, they thought, Jesus is powerful. He can do miracles. So they cheered for Jesus. They waved palm branches. They threw down their coats.

But Jesus did not come to be an earthly king. He came to be our Savior. So, on Good Friday, Jesus died on the cross. And that is when He really saved all people from sin and every evil. On Easter, Jesus showed that He is alive. He showed that He had won a victory over sin, death, and the devil. This is how Jesus helped us. This is how He rescued us.

We can cheer for Jesus too. We can wave palm branches. We can shout "Hosanna!" for Jesus is our Savior King. He is Lord of everything.

6

Find Out More

Why did Jesus ride into Jerusalem on a donkey?

Zechariah is a book in the Old Testament.
In Zechariah 9:9, there is a prophesy about Jesus.
It says a king will enter Jerusalem riding on a donkey.
He will be lowly and humble, like the animal. Jesus
fulfilled (made it come true) that prophesy.

Say It

*Hosanna! Blessed is He who comes in the name
of the Lord.*

John 12:13

Do It

Have your own parade for Jesus. Wave something.
Sing praises to your Savior King.

"Hosanna in the highest!" That ancient song we sing;
For Christ is our Redeemer, The Lord of heav'n our King.
Oh, may we ever praise Him With heart and life and voice
And in His blissful presence Eternally rejoice!

(*LSB* 443:3)

Pray It

Praise God by naming the good things He has done for you.

I wonder, why did someone as important as Jesus wash His disciples' feet?

What jobs do you think are important? Name a few. You probably did not say washing feet. Now we will find out what Jesus thought was important.

On the night before He was arrested, Jesus ate a special meal with His disciples. During the evening, Jesus got up and put a towel around His waist. Then He poured water into a basin (a kind of bowl) and started washing His disciples' feet.

Because people wore sandals and walked on dusty roads, their feet were often dirty. So washing them was not a strange thing to do. What was strange, though, was that Jesus, the Lord and Savior of all, was doing it. Usually, a servant did this job, not the king of heaven and earth.

When Jesus finished, He told His friends why He had washed their feet. He said that no one is greater than another. Jesus wanted His disciples to love and serve others.

The day after that foot-washing lesson, Jesus became the greatest servant ever. He died on the cross for the sins of all people. Later, Jesus' disciples remembered Jesus' lesson. They continued to love and serve others. And so can you!

Find Out More

Did Jesus wash the feet of Judas?
Yes, He did. Jesus washed the feet of
Judas Iscariot, even though He knew Judas
would betray Him.

Say It

Through love serve one another. Galatians 5:13

Do It
Fill a basin with water. Wash and dry the feet of someone else.
Rub them with sweet-smelling lotion. Think about Jesus' teaching.

Pray It
Thank God that His Son, Jesus,
served you by being your Savior. Ask God to
give you a happy heart as you serve others.

I wonder, what is so special about the Lord's Supper?

If you could pick two foods to share with others every year on your birthday, what would they be? Maybe pizza and cake? If so, then eating pizza and cake year after year would become a tradition.

The people of God have traditions. Long ago, on the night before He died, Jesus and His disciples ate a meal where God chose the foods. It was not a birthday meal. It was a meal eaten to remember how God had rescued His people when they were slaves in Egypt. And that night (the night before Jesus died), Jesus also started something new. Jesus picked bread and wine as the special foods. He said the disciples should eat the bread. It was His body. And they should do it to remember Him. Then He took the cup of wine. He said it was His blood. He said they should drink it and remember Him. This meal is known as the Lord's Supper.*

God's people still share the Lord's Supper. They remember Jesus' words. But the Lord's Supper is more than a "remember meal"; it is a Sacrament. In it, the people of God receive forgiveness of sins, life, and salvation. In it, two ordinary foods become special and extraordinary. What makes the meal so special? God does!

*The Lord's Supper is also known as Holy Communion or the Sacrament of the Altar.

Find Out More

What is a sacrament?

A sacrament is a sacred (holy and blessed) act. It began with God. In it, God Himself joins His Word of promise to a visible element. In the Lord's Supper, the bread and wine are the visible elements. In the sacrament, God gives the forgiveness of sins and life eternal.

Say It

Jesus took bread . . . and said, "Take, eat; this is My body." And He took a cup, . . . saying, "Drink of it, all of you, for this is My blood of the covenant,* which is poured out for many for the forgiveness of sins."

Matthew 26:26–28

Do It

Talk about the Lord's Supper. How does your church celebrate this meal? What do you see? What is not seen but is there too?

Pray It

Ask God to forgive your sins for Jesus' sake and to help you love others.

*In these Bible passages, the word *covenant* means "a promise made by God."

I wonder, what did Jesus do in the Garden of Gethsemane?

What happens if you do not feel brave? Maybe you must walk into a dark room alone. Or maybe the sight of dark clouds and the sound of thunder give you the shivers. When you must be brave, do you pray and ask God for help?

On the night before He died, Jesus knew He had to do hard things. He knew He would be arrested. He knew He would be punished. He knew He would die for the sins of all. So what did Jesus do? Jesus led His disciples to the Garden of Gethsemane so He could pray and pray and pray some more. He asked for strength to do what His Father wanted. He asked for help to do His Father's will.

And just after Jesus finished praying, do you know what happened? Along came Judas to betray Jesus. Along came soldiers with torches, clubs, and swords. Along came angry church leaders. And right there in that garden, they arrested Jesus.

When you have something hard to do, you can pray to your heavenly Father too. God will help you do hard things. He will help you say no to temptation. He will help you live as His child.

Find Out More

Who betrayed (was not loyal to) Jesus?

The chief priests and teachers of the Law wanted to get rid of Jesus. They were looking for help. Judas, who was one of Jesus' disciples, heard this and agreed to help. Judas came with Jesus' enemies to the Garden of Gethsemane. He kissed Jesus so the soldiers would know which man to arrest. For this deed, Judas received thirty pieces of silver.

Say It

[Jesus said,] "My Father, if it be possible, let this cup* pass from Me; nevertheless, not as I will, but as You will."

Matthew 26:39

*In this passage, the word *cup* means Jesus' suffering and death.

Do It

Sing the hymn "Go to Dark Gethsemane." Then find your own place to pray.

Go to dark Gethsemane, All who feel the tempter's pow'r;
Your Redeemer's conflict see, Watch with Him one bitter hour;
Turn not from His griefs away; Learn from Jesus Christ to pray.

(*LSB* 436:1)

Pray It

Ask God to help you when you are tempted.

I wonder, what did people think Jesus had done wrong?

Do you like to pretend to be someone else? Do you like to wear a cape, wave a wand, destroy evil?

When Jesus did miracles and told people He was God, some people had faith in Him, but others did not. Some important church leaders thought Jesus was pretending and lying. "How could He be God?" they wondered. So the leaders planned to get rid of Jesus. They had Him arrested and put on trial for saying He was God. Then they tied Jesus up like He was a bad guy, and they took Him to Pilate, the ruler. When Pilate asked Jesus questions, Jesus was mostly silent. Jesus knew what He had to do. Pilate sent Jesus to the soldiers, and they made fun of Him. They dressed Him in a purple robe. They put a crown of thorns on His head. They even beat Him and spit on Him. Then Pilate offered the crowds a chance to set free either Jesus or a prisoner named Barabbas. The crowds chose Barabbas. Finally, Pilate sentenced Jesus to death.

What had Jesus done wrong? Nothing. Jesus' arrest, trial, and death were all unfair. We are the ones who did the wrong things. These things happened so that God could forgive our sins. He sent His Son to earth to be our Savior. He is the perfect sacrifice, the Lamb of God who is pure and holy. What a great big love God has for His children.

14

Find Out More

Who was that man named Barabbas?

Barabbas was a prisoner who was released instead of Jesus. After Pilate talked to Jesus, he did not think Jesus had done anything wrong enough to be killed. Following a custom, Pilate asked a crowd whom he should set free. Was it to be Barabbas, a murderer? Or Jesus, the innocent? The crowd chose the murderer to be free. When asked what to do with Jesus, the crowds answered, "Crucify Him!"

Say It

For our sake He [God] made Him [Jesus] to be sin who knew no sin, so that in Him we might become the righteousness of God.

2 Corinthians 5:21

Do It Draw a crown of thorns. Draw a royal crown. Remember that Jesus is both your Savior and King.

Pray It Thank God that Jesus was willing to suffer for your sake. Ask God to bless believers in Jesus who are suffering for their faith.

15

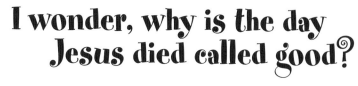

I wonder, why is the day Jesus died called good?

Put on your thinking cap. Think about how something bad can also be something good. Imagine you have a cut knee. Ouch! Cut knees hurt, right? But you can put a Band-Aid on the sore. That is good. And God gave you skin that can heal. That is good.

Now, think about the bad and good of Good Friday. That day, the soldiers nailed Jesus to a cross. That day, the sky turned dark. That day, the curtain tore in the temple. That day, Jesus said, "It is finished," and died.

Jesus died for our sins—for us. That makes us want to cry. We are sorry for the wrong things we think and say and do. But at the same time, we are also happy that Jesus was willing to die on the cross for us. We rejoice. We are excited that He won the victory over sin, death, and the devil. We are thankful that He is the Lamb of God, pure and holy.

So that is why the day Jesus died on the cross is a sad day but a sad day we call good. God's people know Easter is coming. And that is *really* good!

Find Out More

**How do people remember
Jesus' death on Good Friday?**

Churches around the world have
special worship services on Good Friday.
One special service is called a Tenebrae. That is
a Latin word that means "darkness." During this
service, we hear the seven last words that Jesus spoke
from the cross. After each reading, the flame of one
of seven candles is put out. After the last reading, the
last candle is carried out. Then a loud noise is heard. It
represents the closing of Jesus' tomb. The seventh candle
is returned to the chancel to remind us of the Easter joy
to come!

Do It Make the sign of the cross on your
head and heart. Jesus died for you!

Pray It Pray that the people in your family
will believe in Jesus as their Savior from sin.

Say It

The blood of Jesus His Son cleanses us from all sin.
1 John 1:7

I wonder, what happened to Jesus' body after He died?

Do you like to pretend? Do you ever pretend to say good-bye? Do you ever make believe you are going away, so you pretend to grab your keys and backpack? You wave good-bye and pretend to go out the door. It is fun to go away. But maybe instead, you pretend that someone you love is going away. You pretend to open the door for the person. You wave good-bye. You pretend to close the door. You feel sad.

After Jesus died, His friends had to say good-bye to their leader and friend. It was sad for them. Their hearts were hurting. They wanted to show their love for Jesus. They wanted to care for His lifeless body. So a rich man named Joseph asked Pilate for the body of Jesus. Joseph wrapped Jesus' body in a linen cloth and laid it in a new tomb. He rolled a great stone in front of the opening. Nearby, Mary Magdalene and Jesus' mother watched. After he laid Jesus' body to rest, Joseph went home sad. The women went home too, but they planned to return a few days later and put spices on Jesus' lifeless body.

Sunday, when they returned, the women did not need the spices. The lifeless body of Jesus was not there. And their sad good-byes turned to joy.

Find Out More

Who else helped bury Jesus?

In John 19:38–42, we read that Nicodemus (the man who came to Jesus with questions one night) was also there. He brought a sweet-smelling mixture of myrrh and aloes. Luke 23:55 tells us the women who had come with Jesus from Galilee were there too.

Say It

Christ died for our sins in accordance with the Scriptures.

1 Corinthians 15:3

Do It Sing this hymn.

Were you there when
 they crucified my Lord?
Were you there when they crucified
 my Lord?
Oh . . . Sometimes it causes me to
 tremble, tremble, tremble.
Were you there when they crucified my Lord?

Were you there when they nailed Him to the tree?
Were you there when they nailed Him to the tree?
Oh . . . Sometimes it causes me to tremble, tremble, tremble.
Were you there when they nailed Him to the tree?

Were you there when they laid Him in the tomb?
Were you there when they laid Him in the tomb?
Oh . . . Sometimes it causes me to tremble, tremble, tremble.
Were you there when they laid Him in the tomb? (*LSB* 456:1–3)

Pray It

Ask God to be with people who are sad (grieving) because someone they love has died.

I wonder, were there surprises on Easter morning?

Oh, yes! There were many surprises on Easter morning, and they began early at Jesus' tomb. First, an earthquake shook things, and a real angel rolled back the stone. Some soldiers saw what happened. They trembled in fear and ran away. Later, when Mary Magdalene and another Mary arrived with spices for Jesus' body, an angel surprised them too. The angel said Jesus had risen.

"What?" they wondered. "How could it be?" So the women peeked in the tomb to see. And it was true. Jesus was not there. The angel told the women to go and tell the disciples the glad and happy news. So they did. But along the way, they had another surprise. There was Jesus, right in front of them! He said, "Greetings!" At this, the women fell at Jesus' feet and worshiped Him. Now, Jesus wanted them to get up, get going, and tell others that He was alive. And that is just what they did.

What surprises you about the first Easter? Is it that Jesus is alive? Is it that He defeated your enemies—sin, death, and the devil? Or is it that Jesus is the victorious Lamb of God? Whatever it is, may you find joy in believing it and telling others.

He Is Risen !

Find Out More

Why were there guards at the tomb?

Jesus' enemies asked for permission to put guards at the tomb. They were afraid someone would steal Jesus' body and say He had risen from the dead.

Say It

The angel said . . . , "Do not be afraid, for I know that you seek Jesus who was crucified. He is not here, for He has risen, as He said." Matthew 28:5–6

Do It Ring some bells and sing this hymn.

Jesus Christ is ris'n today, Al-le-lu-ia!
Our triumphant holy day, Al-le-lu-ia!
Who did once upon the cross, Al-le-lu-ia!
Suffer to redeem our loss. Al-le-lu-ia!

Hymns of praise then let us sing, Al-le-lu-ia!
Unto Christ, our heav'nly king, Al-le-lu-ia!
Who endured the cross and grave, Al-le-lu-ia!
Sinners to redeem and save. Al-le-lu-ia! (*LSB* 457:1–2)

Pray It Rejoice in Jesus' resurrection, and pray for Him to come again!

I wonder, what do butterflies have to do with Easter?

Hook your thumbs together and flap your fingers. Did you make something that looks like a butterfly?

Butterflies go through a life cycle. There are four stages, from egg to caterpillar to chrysalis to adult. Once the butterfly comes out of its tomb-like home, it is free. It can fly. It is full of life. A butterfly is a good symbol for Jesus' resurrection and the new life we have in Christ.

On that first Easter morning, Mary Magdalene thought Jesus was dead. She went to the tomb early and saw that the stone was not in front of the tomb. She was sad and cried. Then Mary saw two angels. She said, "They have taken away my Lord, and I do not know where they have laid Him" (John 20:13).

Mary turned and saw a man. She thought the man was a worker in the garden. But it was really Jesus. He called her by name, and then she knew Him and worshiped Him. Soon she hurried to tell the disciples the good news that Jesus was alive. She said, "I have seen the Lord" (John 20:18).

Jesus lives. That proves He has defeated our enemies—sin, death, and the devil.

Jesus lives. That means God will forgive our sins.

Jesus lives. This means we will live with Him, now and forever.

Put your thumbs together, make a butterfly, and think about that.

22

Find Out More

What is another Easter symbol?

Easter lilies are a flower used in churches on Easter. The flowers are shaped like trumpets. Trumpets make a loud, happy sound. The lily flowers are also pure white. White reminds us that Jesus was holy. The flowers come to life from a dead-looking bulb.

Say It

[Jesus said,] "Because I live, you also will live."
John 14:19

Do It

Say this traditional Easter greeting to one another. One person says, "The Lord is risen!" The other says, "He is risen indeed!" Try it out!

Pray It

Thank Jesus for His victory over your enemies. When you finish your prayer, do a cheer!

I wonder, were there Easter eggs on that first Easter?

Today, most children get all kinds of Easter eggs on Easter morning. But what happened on that first Easter?

That morning, Peter and another disciple ran to the tomb to check out a story. They had heard from some women that Jesus was not there. But they did not believe it. They knew Jesus' lifeless body had been sealed in the tomb. So how could He not be there? They ran to the tomb to see for themselves. And what do you think? It was true; the tomb was empty. Then they believed the women.

"But what about the Easter eggs?" you wonder. How do they go along with the Easter story? Long ago, the hard shell of the eggs reminded people of Jesus' tomb—the one that was sealed shut. And cracking that shell open reminded them that Jesus did not stay in the tomb. Instead, He rose from the dead. So the egg became a good symbol of Jesus' resurrection.

Enjoy your Easter eggs. And as you open them, think of the glorious resurrection and the empty tomb! Then open your Bible to read about that first Easter. Think about how you can believe in Jesus. You believe because God has given you faith in Baptism and through His Word. And through faith, you believe the tomb is empty. You believe in the resurrection of the dead and in life everlasting.

Find Out More

What did Jesus do when He was made alive?

The Bible tells us that Jesus descended into hell to proclaim His victory over His enemies.

Say It

[Jesus said,] "I am the resurrection and the life."
John 11:25

Do It

Use different-colored Easter eggs (plastic or colored on paper) to help you tell the Easter story.

Pray It

Thank God that He has given you faith to believe that Jesus lives. Pray for those who do not yet believe in Jesus.

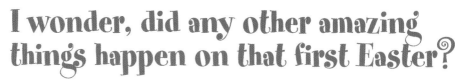

I wonder, did any other amazing things happen on that first Easter?

You already know some amazing things about Easter.

- Jesus rose from the dead.
- An angel rolled the stone away.
- Some men and women saw the empty tomb.
- Some women even saw Jesus.

But wait; there's more!

On that day, two sad disciples were walking to the town of Emmaus from Jerusalem. As they walked along, they talked about Jesus' death and other things that had happened. Soon, another man joined them. It was Jesus, but the two men were kept from recognizing Him.

Jesus asked the men why they were sad. They said they had hoped Jesus was the Savior, but His body was missing. Then Jesus explained God's Word. He told them why the Christ had to suffer to be the Savior.

When they got to Emmaus, it was getting late. The men asked Jesus to stay, and He agreed. While they were eating, Jesus blessed the bread and broke it. At once, the eyes of the men were opened and they recognized Jesus. Then Jesus vanished.

So what did they do with this good news? They ran all the way back to Jerusalem. They found the disciples and said, "The Lord has risen indeed" (Luke 24:34). Now, that is another amazing thing!

We can ask Jesus to help us understand His Word too. And here is one more amazing thing. He gives us His Holy Spirit to help us do just that.

Find Out More

Where does faith come from?

Faith is a gift of the Holy Spirit. In Baptism and through His Word, God gives us faith to believe in Him as our Savior.

Say It

The Lord has risen indeed.

Luke 24:34

Do It

Make a Bible by putting your hands together.

Open the Bible and say these words.

The Bible tells me of God's love.
It says God sent His only Son
To earth to save me from my sin,
And through His death, forgiveness win.

Close the Bible and say these words.

The Bible tells me I can go
And show God's love to those I know.
And as I go, God goes with me,
For I am His child, redeemed and free.

Pray It

Ask God to help you learn His Word.

I wonder, when did the disciples first see Jesus alive?

On Easter evening, most of the disciples were together with the doors locked. Suddenly, Jesus appeared, standing with them. He said, "Peace be with you" (John 20:19). But His friends were still afraid. So Jesus showed them the wounds in His hands and side. Then the disciples saw that Jesus was a living person. He was not a ghost. It was true, they thought—it was the Lord.

Jesus' friends had questions. They wondered why He, their teacher and friend, had to suffer and die. Jesus explained why these things had to happen for Him to be the Savior of all. With His help, the disciples believed.

Then Jesus gave His disciples a job as His witnesses. He wanted them to tell what they had seen and heard. He wanted them to explain God's Word.

When did you first hear about Jesus? Maybe it was when someone told you or read you a Bible story. Or maybe when someone sang you a song. Maybe someone took you to church to receive God's gifts through His Word and Sacraments.

God's family grows like that, one by one. The work of telling others about Jesus continues through God's children of all ages, even you.

He Is Risen !

Find Out More

Who can help us understand God's Word?

God has given you His Holy Spirit to help you. He has also given you loving and caring adults—parents, teachers, and pastors.

Say It

Thanks be to God, who gives us the victory through our Lord Jesus Christ.

1 Corinthians 15:57

Do It

Make someone a card to tell the Easter story.

Pray It

Pray for those who preach and teach God's Word.

I wonder, where is Jesus now?

After Easter, Jesus used His divine attributes to help His followers believe in Him. To do that, He showed that He really was alive. And He showed that He really was God.

After forty days, Jesus was ready to return to His Father. He met His disciples on a mountain in Galilee. He said to them, "Go therefore and make disciples of all nations, baptizing them in the name of the Father and of the Son and of the Holy Spirit, teaching them to observe all that I have commanded you. And behold, I am with you always, to the end of the age" (Matthew 28:19–20).

Right then, right there, Jesus sent His disciples to make more disciples. They were to use God's tools—His Word and Baptism. And Jesus said they would not be alone. He would be with them always.

Now Jesus was ready to ascend into heaven. Slowly He rose, and a cloud covered Him. Then, the Bible tells us He sat down at the right hand of God the Father. And from there, He rules.

"Where is Jesus now?" you wonder. He ascended to reign, and He is also with His children. Through faith, we believe these two things can be true. We believe He is the victorious Lamb of God. And we believe He is with us too!

Find Out More

What is Jesus doing for me now?
He rules and reigns for you.
He is Lord of heaven and earth.
And He is with you. He is present
in His Word and Sacraments.

Say It

[God] raised Him [Jesus] from the dead and seated Him at His right hand in the heavenly places. Ephesians 1:20

Do It

Make up a melody and sing the word *alleluia.* Then praise God with singing. And if you like, use instruments too!

Pray It

Ask God to help you serve Him faithfully all the days of your life. And when your days on earth shall end, ask Him to give you joy and peace.

I wonder, what happened after Jesus ascended into heaven?

After Jesus ascended into heaven, the disciples gathered in a room and waited for the gift of the Holy Spirit. It came ten days later, on Pentecost. It came with the sound of a rushing wind. It came with what appeared to be fire on the heads of the disciples. It came and gave the disciples the ability to speak in many languages about Jesus' life, death, and resurrection.

The Holy Spirit is still working. He comes to people of all ages in a different way than He did on that first Pentecost. He comes through God's Word, spoken and read. He comes in His Sacraments. Through these Means of Grace, the Holy Spirit calls people of all ages to a true and living faith in Jesus Christ.

Those who believe are bold to confess their faith in the words of the Apostles' Creed. You can do that at church with others. But you can also do it right now, with those gathered around you. Try it. Together, say the words of the Second Article. Tell what Jesus has done for you!

Apostles' Creed
The Second Article

I believe in . . .
Jesus Christ, His [God's] only Son, our Lord,
who was conceived by the Holy Spirit, born of
the Virgin Mary, suffered under Pontius Pilate,
was crucified, died, and was buried. He descended
into hell. The third day He rose again from the dead.
He ascended into heaven and sits at the right hand
of God, the Father Almighty. From thence He will
come to judge the living and the dead.

This is most certainly true.